Brooklyn's Autumn Dusk

Barbara Staten

BookLeaf
Publishing
India | USA | UK

Presentation by *BookLeaf Publishing*

Web: www.bookleafpub.com

E-mail: info@bookleafpub.com

ISBN: 9789360948108

First edition 2024

*This book is dedicated to my niece
LaToneya, and a host of friends that
encouraged me and listened to my poems
for they knew that my soul was talking out
loud.*

Autumn Dusk In Brooklyn

Burnt orange burst into view.
Amidst the Indigo sky
Summons by Oya to look up.
As the autumn leaves of the bald Cypress trees
came into view
A Hip Hop dance battle ensued.
Propelled by the wind.
As the row of trees aligned parallel to my
elementary school
Competed for my attention.
Exchange of energy occurred.
As I felt the heartbeat of the carbon absorbing,
oxygen producing
Consciousness commune with me.
Experiencing ecstasy
Knowing and feeling the oneness of all.
Walking in the jungle of concrete
The wind sang, the sirens screamed, the dog
barked and
The leaves of the bald Cypress trees
Danced amidst the indigo sky.

North Country

Gifted with a ride to the North country,
To breathe, clear my mind and set my spirit free.
The trees greeted me with their majestic colors
of Autumn's song.
And the Catskills and Adirondack mountains
loomed on the horizon as if to contain my fragile
existence.
Beautiful, strong, humble, authentic Black Men
of my bloodline catered to my every need.
And the Canadian geese sang their morning cry
as they flew high with the eternal message of
keep your head to the sky.
HBO "Lovecraft" illuminated the ills of this
reality.
The three-point two-mile trail revealed the
stamina within that covid 19 attempted to steal.
Four-legged companion galloped after marking
the landscape.
The misty fog baptism prepared the wounded
healer to return to the suspended, traumatized
city of stoned hearts and concrete.
A kind familiar provided a hot meal and artistic
gifts of crystal and acrylic abstracts along the
journey home.

The plants on the porch maintained their life force.
And I settled in to watch the Deacons for Defense.
As the lines to vote extended for blocks, the virus continued to spread, and the stimulus package was stalled.

Bird On A Wire

Raven sits on a wire
Surveilling the landscape below
To plot and plan his strategy,
Of conquering the social constructs
That binds him to the demons within.
With keen sight and intellect
He flies from high mounts to low valleys.
In search of his true self actualization
Moving through multiple dimensions
And multiple dwellings to find refuge.
Aware of the duality, he embraces the feminine
And receives the nurturance of the yearning
child.
Implementation creates manifestation,
Of the denied and deferred dreams
Now Raven sits on a wire
Overlooking the beautiful bountifulness
That he has created in this third dimensional
reality.

ALOHA HAWAII

Aloha Hawaii with tears and tears in my heart.
HO'OPONOPONO prayer for the ancient
mountain top land mass of sunken Lumeria
You Hawaii, Big Island demonstrates the eternal,
volcanic, biochemical life force of Gaia, Mother
Earth
You Hawaii, represents paradise found and
paradise lost.
The native people have given their blood to
preserve the sacred land and righteous way to be
on Gaia.
All opposing values have consumed the
bountifulness and choked the breath of the land
with Cell towers, Electric grids, skyscrapers,
greed, capitalism and human misery.
You Hawaii, now summons Pele to release the
elements of wind and fire to
Sacrifice Lanaian of Maui
One of your beloved children, a historical town
that preserves the stories and
Holds the legacy.
To warn humanity that time is up.
Change, open your heart or be demolished.
Aloha Hawaii you will heal.
For you have been here for eons
And the Banyan tree still stands.

THE OTHER

I exist therefore I am.
You cannot eliminate or cancel me
With your lies and hatred.
I am you in a polarized form or mirror image
Of the parts of your own self-hatred and fear.
From the broken parts of your wounded psyche.
Embrace the shadow cast by the light of a
trillion atomic explosions occurring within
Every time I come into view or thought.
A million AR 15s will never destroy me.
Instead, expand my DNA into the cosmos to be
absorbed
By new souls coming through
So, stop all this foolishness of self-hatred in the
form of projected identification.
We are one living on Mother Earth.
Feed the hungry
House the homeless
Care for the sick
Keep the children safe
Protect Mother Earth
Only take what you need.

DEN OF SIN

We all visit the den of sin
To feed the flesh and ego
While existing in this human form
Enticing, erotic, stimulation of
Nerves, Neurons and Nipples
The purple haze of multiple smokables
Spins us into a trance as we move through
Dimensions with no desire to return to our
former state.
The willingness to neglect all,
Commitments and responsibilities.
And allow the teeth, the hair, the body
To wither away without notice.
There are no guides or protectors once
We enter the den of sin
Our souls have been captured.
Only the prayers of our loved ones can
Free us from the den of sin

COOPER THE COCKAPOO

Dog gone but not for long.
Someone stole my cockapoo.
In New York City, that's what they do.
First, I was sad and mad, then shed a tear.
Then I was glad cause I remembered what My
Reverend E said,
Nothing is lost, if it is yours, it will come back to
you.
So, I said a prayer and headed home.
In front of my gate Cooper appeared
Traumatized dirty and full of despair.
He signaled to feed him, give him water and
leave him alone.
For he was tired and glad to be home
He telepathically told me what occurred.
They put him in a dirty van, and he bit them on
the hand feet and face.
So, they threw him out of that place.
He landed on his back in a pool of muddy, oily
water.
Once composed he crossed the streets with focus
and order.
With his keen sense of smell
My cockapoo came home.
So now we will never be alone.

MOTHER'S DAY

Embrace the soul that chose to occupy
Your womb for nine months
Feel the biochemical changes as the
Spiritual entity develops into material
manifestation.
Prepare to experience unconditional love
As you feel the kick, hear the heartbeat and see
the image
While rubbing your swollen belly
Breath, Push, Scream, Contract, Expand
To release the child into this dimension
Care and nurture this child of the universe
Lead and guide him or her to a purposeful life
Of this souls' destiny
Redirect when lead astray
Encourage acts of kindness, virtue and self-love
Always pray for your child's protection
As they journey on planet earth
For you have given yourself and this child
The greatest gift of experiencing pure
unconditional love.
Babies breathe fills spaces
With divine love and healing
Bring heaven to earth.

HOMECOMING TO ZULU LAND

I've long for you for 400 years
When we were separated by the colonists
Who captured me and repressed my culture, my
language
And my true sense of self
I've been with you in dreamland.
And felt your heartbeat during the drumming in
the woods of Louisiana,
And echoing sounds of the winds of Oya.
I've cheered for you watching Shaka Zulu movie
on the big screen, hearing Steve Biko's speeches
and singing Nelson Mandela's freedom songs.
Now I have found you traveling 10,000 miles.
To retrieve my culture, my language and my true
sense of self.
Thank you for waiting for me and
Welcoming your Queen home.
I offer you blankets for your family and
ancestors to provide comfort, warmth and
blessings.
I place currency in the belly of the sacred cow to
prove my love and loyalty to you.
I sing and dance in jubilation expressing the joy
in my heart and soul.

This is our day to show, to share and to signify
Black Love.

SIRENS IN EAST FLATBUSH

The sirens echo through the empty streets every
five minutes.
As if a divine alarm is set to take another soul.
To the isolation tank at the nearest hospital,
To petition for more time on earth
While being suffocated by an invisible
Electromagnetic biosynthetic poison.
This task you must do alone
Whispers the spirit guides and ancestors.
For your spouse, partner, children or friends
Cannot enter the portal with you.
Your deeds and fears will be reviewed.
And the choice you alone will make.
Stay on this plane of joy and pain.
Or release the spirit to return to the eternal
divine source.

A POEM FOR MICHAEL THE ACTOR

Michael you are my magical elixir.
A potion I can only drink in small amounts.
Yet, I crave for your presence daily.
And curse the Gods for creating barriers of
separation.
Your deep voice opens the dark chambers of my
soul.
A familiar sound from the belly of the slave
ships
Where our ancestors secretly nurtured seeds of
freedom
Through voice and song.
Your touch sends chills up and down my spine to
clear the blocked chakras.
Your strong arms embracing my fragile body
fills me with courage to carry on.
I search playhouses throughout the land
With the hope of experiencing the essence of
you absorbed by the audience.
 I will think of you.
Then dream of you.
To drink of your magical elixir eternally.

MANGO AT MIDNIGHT

He brings me a mango at midnight.
I quietly open the front door to my heart.
To embrace the fullness of his essence
And relieve the stress and fear of my existence.

He brings me a mango at midnight.
As I taste the fruits and juices of the Caribbean
islands
And seek out the souls of my kin folks from the
four-hundred-year separation.

He brings me a mango at midnight.
Knowing we are too old for a traditional
relationship.
Thus, only meet up when the moon is full and
the earth is quiet.
So, the darkness will contain our secret.

He brings me a mango at midnight.
Then disappears at the break of dawn.
Leaving me content and contained to tolerant
The stress and fear of my existence

Until the next full moon, the midnight, the
mango, and the man merges
Hence, he will bring me a mango at midnight.

INAUGURATION 2021

On this day the sacred prevails and the profane
Fades into the background of the woods and
wilderness
Of this great land to resolve the hate that runs
through their blood
And reflect on the defeated leader that led them
astray.
Yes, a new day has dawn, and it is quiet at the
capitol.
No hundreds of thousands citizens welcoming
the New Elected President
Who achieved his goal on a third charm
And choose Kamala of Afro Jamaican and East
Indian genotype.
And female gender as his Vice President
For balance and representation of all
Those who came and those who viewed through
various electronics
Hold hope in their hearts for a more perfect
union.
And faith that compassion, competence,
cooperation and coordination could contain the
covid virus that has claimed 400,000 as of
1/20/2021 /one million plus by 2023 souls.

Who show their presence at the sacred ritual
with the waving of multiple
American flags on the Capitol lawn propelled by
Oya the African Orisha of the wind greeting the
deceased.
The leaders greet each other with their eyes for
their faces are covered with protective masks of
many colors like the people of the land.
The eyes twinkle with a gleam of relief that the
democracy has been saved.
And can no longer be taken for granted.
So, let God bless America with amazing grace to
heal and restoreth its soul.

WALKING GENTLY IN PARADISE

In paradise you can walk gently
Each step is light as if levitating
All elements in harmony
As your heart rate is at rest
And all thoughts of fear and hatred disappear
In paradise the sun activates
Your melanated cells and stimulates vitamin D
Til you become the bronzed illuminated one
To reflect the oneness of all beings
In paradise the ocean of Yemaya sings you
Into a deep trance like sleep
Where you dream of past lives and lovers
And the childhood traumas are released
In paradise the ancestors visit you
As winged and amphibian companions
Reminding you of the beauty and blessing of
living in this present
Physical form
In paradise beautiful, bold, voluptuous, Black
women
Can embrace their right
To exist, to exhale, to excel and
To expand to rewrite their story.

WINTER ON THE HORIZON

The golden amber leaves are illuminated by the
faded light of dusk.
As if holding on to the last of the absorbed
summer's sunlight.
With each rainstorm the tree branches become
naked and bare.
Sprinkling the dull gray concrete with golden
amber leaves.
Autumn comes in waves.
Fluctuating temperatures
Allowing open toe sandals with overcoats and
scarfs.
The darkness greets you in the morn and the cell
phones illumination guides the
Afterschool students to their tenement doorsteps
Barbecue jerk chicken grills line the avenues.
As the smells of McDonald's fries, popeye's
chicken and Dunkin donut coffee,
Distracts the senses from the mountains of
black, plastic garbage bags.
Feeding grounds for the other mammal city
dwellers.
The undocumented Mayans Mexicans
Guatemalans and El Salvadoran

Hastily build new condos at every vacant lot
To complete the city's gentrification plan
Before the first snow
I go within closing the heavy velvet curtains.
Stocking up on beans and good books
Reflecting on summer's lover and retreating
from the world in
Preparation for winter

EMPTY HOUSE

The house is empty now
No longer echoing the pitter patter of little feet
Running up and down the stairs
The walls no longer hold the smells of salmon
cakes, peas and rice or
Fried whittlings every Friday
And Chittlings, Black eye peas and greens every
New Years eve

The house is empty now
No more poker and spades card games in the
dining room til 4am
Aretha Franklin blasting on the CD player or the
Price is Right blaring
On the 70-inch TV that consumes the living
room

The house is empty now
No more New Years Eve parties during
snowstorms
Block buster's movies night
Latest model Cadillac parked in the front
Or extended family members gatherings every
holiday

The porch is empty now
Granny no longer sits on the porch
Wearing her hand made dresses while greeting
the passer bys with a hi shug

Big Frank early bird friends have flew away
losing their bird feeder
Who drank his coffee while visualizing the
dollars he would earn that day
While doing the New York hustle

The Chinese restaurant across the street has
closed
And the replaced jerk chicken spot didn't last
one year due to Covid
The exterior red paint is peeling and
The concrete walkway is crumbling.
The windows hold ten years of dust and the
colossal red rose bush withered away After the
last long-term resident died

A new resident has moved into the empty house
She holds the memories joys and pains of the
house
And through a five-year cleansing ritual
absorbed digested and regurgitated the traumas
and toxins that the walls and floors hold

She releases the love joys and strength that was
trapped in the crevices of the living room stone
walls.
She exterminates the pest and creatures that
lurks throughout the house during the night
She brings fresh oxygen with her aloe Vera mint
and prayer plants
She reminds the remaining family members to
hold on to the joy strength and nurturing that
they received while being dwellers of the house
To fill the empty house with love once again.

HEALING THE WOUNDS
THAT BIND US

UNCOVER RECOVER DISCOVER
UNCOVER THE PAIN AND TRAUMA THAT
ALLOWS THE SHADOWS TO BLOCK OUR
LIGHT
UNCOVER THE LIES WE BELIEVE ABOUT
OURSELVES THAT STEALS OUR
COURAGE OUR CONFIDENCE AND OUR
FAITH
UNCOVER THE MASKS WE DISPLAY TO
THE WORLD THAT PROJECTS A PSEUDO
SMILE
UNCOVER RECOVER DISCOVER
RECOVER THE CHILD FULL OF
WONDERMENT, RIDING HIS NEW BIKE
ON CHRISTMAS DAY, PLAYING STICK
BALL IN THE STREETS OF NEW YORK
AND MAKING SCOOTERS OUT OF MILK
CRATES
RECOVER THE ALTO SINGER WEARING
FLY CLOTHES AND PLATFORM SNAKE
SKIN SHOES, SINGING THE SONGS OF
THE DRAMATICS, DELFONICS AND
STYLISTICS

RECOVER THE LOVE AND ADMIRATION
OUR CHILDREN OUR FAMILY AND OUR
FRIENDS HOLD FOR US
UNCOVER RECOVER DISCOVER
DISCOVER THE GIFTS BESTOWED UPON
US TO SHARE WITH HUMANITY
DISCOVER A WORLD FULL OF BEAUTY,
PROSPERITY AND GRACE
DISCOVER THE HEALING POWER OF
HEALTHY FOOD, HEALTHY THOUGHTS,
AND CLEAN LIVING
DISCOVER THE HEALER WITHIN EACH
OF US TO COMFORT AND SOOTH OTHERS
WITH OUR CALM PRESENCE, GENTLE
TOUCH, ATTENTIVE GAZE, AND KIND
WORDS
UNCOVER RECOVER DISCOVER THE
ESSENCE OF YOU

MOUNTAIN AS A wITNESS

Superstition Mountain
Bears Witness to a Union of
Two souls full of light and lovingkindness
And the heavenly stars dance and twinkle in
celebration
As Global cultures merge and entangle
In a hypnotic dance while wearing the
Majestic fabrics of ancient times
A hall full of Healers of all disciplines
Humbly express Thanksgiving and
Gratitude for the special invitation
To experience the power of love
And be bathed in their love, their light, and their
lovingkindness.

WE ARE GOD'S LIGHT

Your light is stronger than your shadow.
Your light brings healing and joy to the world.
Your light empowers your children to live their dreams.
Your light holds the family legacy.
Your light has brought others from the shadow of death.
Don't let the shadow consume your light.
For your light is God.

IN A DREAM

In a dream, in a flower, in a dish, in a song
Our loved ones still comfort and guide us.
Although they have moved on

Granny came to me in a dream.
When it was time to leave the California scene
And move back to New York to care for kinfolks
and create new dreams.

Momma appeared in a field of sunflowers that
continued as far as the eye could see
To remind me of my own power and infinity

Daddys dish was salmon cakes
He would make them in the morning with grits
and eggs
What more need be said

Love and Happiness was my only sister's
favorite song.
Every time I hear it on the radio, I know she's
not gone just in another form.

DECADES OF HAIR TEXTURE

I was a dixie peach from Georgia.
Frying up my do with royal crown, bergamont
and blue magic,
To take the grey hound to New York City to seek
my fortune.
So, I processed my conk with lye, and I knew I
was fly and put on my best and you know the
rest,
Uptown on the A train
Oh my God it was insane!
Got some knowledge from the Moslem brother
and the five percenter.
Then went to Sylvia's for dinner.
Saw Smokey, Supremes and Marvin at the
Apollo
In the crowd there was no sorrow.
Black power was in the air and there was no
fear.
Rap Brown said burn nigga burn.
And the Black Panthers carried arms in the air.
Then, Malcolm, King and Medger were slayed
And our people felt lots of pain
So we threw away the royal crown.
Held up our fists with dashikis and afros

and we marched to the beat of James Brown,
Mayfield and Sly
Singing no justice, no peace and this is no lie.
Then the cocaine crack and aids
made our dreams fade.
And we fell into a slumber,
Waiting for the Trumpeter.
Obama appeared out of thin air.
That's when the people locked their hair to
retrieve their power
During this transformative hour.
And we cried cause our savior was here.
Give the people their rights.
Obama care was passed.
But the republicans put up a fight and acted like
an ass.
They took over the senate and thne put a maniac
in the executive chair.
He who hated everyone who's skin was not fair.
He reigned for four years.
Leaving with two impeachments and a plague
for us to bear,
500 thousand falling in the east and 500
thousand falling in the west
taking the regular folks and the best.
Young people now wear hairs of others.
Donated to the Temple Goddesses
While refusing the vaccine for the virus that has
killed

their mothers, fathers, sisters, and brother....
to be continued....

www.ingramcontent.com/pod-product-compliance
Lightning Source LLC
Chambersburg PA
CBHW071239140726
47996CB00007B/2675